PRAYERS FOR EVERYDAY THRIVING

GABRIELLE NUMAIR, MA

BLUE WHITE PUBLISHING

COPYRIGHT

Publisher's Note

This publication represents a personal perspective. It is offered and sold with the understanding that neither the author nor publisher is engaged in providing psychological, medical or other professional services. If counseling, medical or other specialized assistance is needed, the services of a competent licensed professional should be engaged.

Blue White Publishing

Copyright©2019 by Gabrielle Numair

All Rights Reserved

No part of this book may be reproduced or transmitted in any form or by any means, electronic or mechanical, including photocopying, recording or by any information storage and retrieval system without written permission from the author.

DEDICATION

To the love that always surrounds us

To the assistance always available

To the choice that is always ours

CONTENTS

1. Introduction — 1
2. TO SUPPORT WELL-BEING — 13
3. Morning Intention #1 — 15
4. Morning Intention #2 — 17
5. Daily Intention for You — 19
6. Daily Intention for Another — 21
7. Bedtime Intention — 23
8. Guidance for You — 25
9. Guidance for Another — 27
10. Expanding Awareness — 29
11. Making Way for My Well-Being — 31
12. Conscious Creator #1 — 33
13. Constancy of Source — 35
14. Directing My Expression — 37
15. Internal Health — 39
16. Tending My Garden — 41
17. Expecting Positive Outcomes — 43
18. Conscious Creator #2 — 45
19. Mastering Constructive Use of My Free Will — 47
20. Life's Goodness — 49
21. Happiness — 51
22. TO SUPPORT EVERYDAY EVENTS — 53
23. Emergencies — 55
24. Transforming a World Crisis — 57
25. Releasing Habits of Fear and Anxiety — 59
26. Growing Cooperative Relationships — 61
27. Attracting a Wonderful New Home — 63
28. Selling a Home/Attracting an Ideal Buyer — 65
29. House Blessing — 67
30. Opening to a New Job — 69
31. Opening to a New Career — 71
32. Launching a Successful Business — 73
33. Sustaining a Successful Business — 75
34. Mindful Conception — 77

35. Mindful Adoption	79
36. TO SUPPORT HEALTH	81
37. Overall Healthy Practices	83
38. Welcoming Vibrant Health	85
39. Transforming the Situation	87
40. Gracious Thanks	89
41. Developing Healthy Expectations	91
42. Blessing of Medicine, Vitamins and Food I	93
43. Blessing of Medicine, Vitamins and Food II	95
44. Blessing of Junk Food	97
45. Healing a Migraine Pattern*	99
46. Creating and Experiencing Vibrant Health/Mastering Vibrant Health	103
47. Easy Add-In Habits	105
48. Notes on Evolving Expectations	107
49. TO SUPPORT ABUNDANCE	109
50. Welcoming Financial Abundance	111
51. Mastering Financial Ease	113
52. Exercising Conscious Creation	115
53. TO SUPPORT A GRACIOUS TRANSITION	117
54. What is meant by a gracious transition?	119
55. Getting Ready Part I	123
56. Getting Ready Part Ii	125
57. For A Loved One	127
58. TO SUPPORT EVOLVING EXPECTATIONS	129
59. Quick Set-Up #1	131
60. Quick Set-Up #2	133
61. Quick Set-Up #3	135
62. Quick Set-Up #4	137
YOUR INSPIRATIONS	138
Inspirations Cont.	139
Inspirations Cont.	140
Inspirations Cont.	141
About the Author	142

ACKNOWLEDGEMENTS

With gratitude for your love, support and inspiration:

R. Brian Keith, PhD, Stephanie Jourdan, PhD, David, Emily, John, CIM Girls (Rozanne, Colleen, Sue, Karen K.), Nazha, Rebekka, Jodie, Arielle, Carol S., Molly, Maria G., Louise Hay, Esther Hicks & Abraham, Ernest Holmes, The Fillmores, Marianne Williamson, A Course in Miracles, Oprah, Edouard, Andillon, Ruthie G., Abraham N., Kallie H., Rich O., Bob S., Donna L., Stan & Julie W., Susan S., Jennifer B., Jon N., Nancy N., Abe & Susan N., Isi & Claus H., Diane & John D., Clyde B., Terry C., Kim & CB, JA, Dottie & Phil W., Janet W., The McGowans, Francesca, Lila N, and my fellow 1992-94 counseling interns and clinical supervisors at the Southern California Counseling Center.

INTRODUCTION

It is said we tend to share what we actively seek to learn.

The prayers, affirmation and focused statements shared here reflect some of my active spiritual practices, a sort of dynamic playbook which has evolved through the days, years and seasons of my life.

Sometimes we can't think straight due to an emotionally trying time and positive prayers seem just beyond our grasp. Sometimes we need a little help in seeing more clearly or in switching our focus. These prayers and affirmations are intended to support you during such times and are also intended to support you in developing constructive habits so that you can more readily realize the positive changes you seek.

Some of these prayers and affirmations will resonate with you and some will not. Use what feels good to you, alter whatever calls out to you and ignore the rest. I hope you are inspired to change everything to better match your needs as a conscious creator of your life and there is space at end of the book in support of this purpose.

As you journey to thrive, I feel it is essential to have the internal honesty to acknowledge and examine the thoughts behind your thoughts and your current expectations that create and perpetuate your experiences. Personal forgiveness is a key in unlocking candid self-awareness – otherwise you are just spinning your wheels and likely shaking your fist at heaven. Be brave; have the courage to look within and commit to a practice of developing your prayers and affirmations to a new level by attentively retraining and redirecting the highways of your mind.

Navigation Bits and Pieces

Prayer/Affirmation/Focused Statement: These terms hold the following implications within this book: intentional direction of free will, declaration of desired outcome, proclamation of direction, assertion of desires, creative focus, in other words, our free will in conscious action.

God/Source/Universe/Life Force/Creative Force: These terms are used interchangeably and are sometimes coupled. As is your preference, insert your favorite naming classification/label for that which created us and connects us all. Don't let your dislike of a term be your excuse for not pursuing your goals. Such subterfuge can be minimized by considerate understanding and acceptance of your internal defense system. Look beyond the labels and utilize the essence contained within the words. Change what does not flow for you and move forward.

Amen/So Be It: These terms are often used together though they hold the same meaning to me. I find an energetic boost when coupling the phrases.

Some of My Journey

I grew up in an extended family with a loving grandmother who had more than the healing touch. A devout Catholic, my grandmother maintained a personal altar and regularly blessed our home with incense from the church. Often we did not need words to communicate.

I was never drawn to traditional religions despite fourteen years of religious education but was definitely aware of my spiritual nature. As an adult, Unity and Centers for Spiritual Living have been most helpful to me along the way.

A child of divorce with an absentee father, I had a few issues to say the least. At fifteen, I started to look into meditation as it filtered into mainstream America in the mid to late 1960's and I was fortunate to attend college during the tremendous social, political and spiritual openings of the time and survived!

Through the decades that followed, I worked, married and divorced twice, raised a child, completed a master's degree in psychology, studied hypnotherapy and other mind-body modalities, had a counseling practice, encountered my share of health, personal and professional challenges and usually continued on my path of spiritual inquiry, personal healing and development. It was not a cake walk. There were many times when I certainly said "enough" and hunkered down wishing for oblivion or worse.

So how did I get to this time and place? With lots of help along the way and somehow getting back on the proverbial horse time and time again by doing my homework. Sounds exciting doesn't it? Unfortunately, I haven't found any secret shortcuts to pass along to you. I have come to realize that homework is an ever evolving constant in a soul's journey. Study, dialogue and self-reflection may bring awareness to developmental areas but there is definitely a time when the rubber needs to meet the road.

Exercising our free will constructively is a choice and it takes a commitment to retrain our set pathways of living. We are blessed to have the option to see and to choose differently. I do hope you find the words here to be practical and helpful as you pray, and on your journey.

An Invitation

> *Walk with me for a bit and discover*
> *if there are any flowers to add to your basket.*

If so, allow yourself the gifts of patience and kindness at the onset of this endeavor. What seems simple often is not easy. There is a reason that Olympic athletics practice so hard and for so long. Why would we expect less of a commitment to retrain and redirect our habits of living toward the directions we desire?

Our current ways of thinking and being did not occur overnight. Our current habits of living (positive and not so positive) were acquired through conscious and unconscious training. Whether our training was received from our family, friends, schools, religion, media, etc., it was training in thoughts, words, feelings, actions and expectations. And we now automatically feel, think, act and broadcast the information and expectations in which we have been instructed.

So at this point, you have an opportunity or yet another opportunity to make the changes you wish to see in your life consciously and purposefully. What does this have to do with prayers and affirmations? – Everything!

We enter and exit this world alone. This work occurs alone within your consciousness. Yes, I feel we are all connected in reality but ultimately the work is yours to do. Hopefully you allow yourself to receive assistance along the way. You may have a counselor, shaman, instructor, minister, guide or other trusted individual in your life who can help you experience a momentary elevated state but you alone exercise your skills in constructive conscious creation.

Counselors, friends, writers, guides, ministers, etc., can show you possibilities and can hold the lantern of hope for you but you have to actively take the torch and run with it at some point. Yes, I used the word "have to" as I do not feel we can really escape the job we have been given: To develop and thrive through positive cultivation of our free will or in other words, to be as God/Source created us to be. We can avoid what I feel is our true job for lifetimes and probably not have a lot of real and sustained happiness in those lifetimes. At some point I feel we must make friends with our destiny as God's offspring and endeavor to live consciously as creators…and for me, this means using our free will consciously and constructively. This is what brings our prayers/affirmations to life.

You have probably heard the phrase, "Every thought is a prayer". Well, what about every word, feeling, action and expectation? Would it take too much effort to pay attention to all of this? This offered way of living might feel like a burden but possibly only because it may be unfamiliar territory. There can be true delight in this undertaking if we would allow it to be so. We are always creating whether consciously or unconsciously. For whatever reason and perhaps mainly due to our prior training, many of us use our free will in not so positive ways. Imagine if we were trained from the time we were born to cultivate our free will in positive ways? Something to consider.

If you are praying for something, you are asking for a change and wanting something different

Are you at a place and time in your life to make some changes in support of your prayers and your life? I hope you will consider this invitation as an opportunity to see differently, to pray differently, to choose differently and to live differently.

Laying the Foundation: Repetition

Many of the statements in the pages ahead are repetitive in nature to assist you in building a new "go-to" thought foundation with the intent to influence your outcomes in a positive manner. With practice, when a significant situation occurs, you need not scurry around because you have established a portfolio of positive anchors through your personal efforts.

For example, it is one thing to study a new language and excel in a controlled classroom environment. But if faced with a critical situation in a foreign country, practiced repetition of and practiced redirection toward the new language are what will see you through. In essence, practice as if you are in a different country with a different language and your survival depended on it. Practice your new thinking, feeling, acting and language tools until they become second nature. **Most importantly, practice managing your expectations which has the most impact on your prayers, affirmations and outcomes.**

It can be helpful to remember a current habit or task that is easy for you. Use what is already easy as a mental trigger and link that feeling of success to whatever you choose to work on. If you want to work on a physical issue, call to mind something that is easy for you physically and link your comfort in this area to the success you want to achieve in your current area of physical need. Support your desired changes with your thoughts, words, actions, feelings and expectations.

If you are someone who recovers quickly from a cold after a good night's sleep… this is something that you know is easy for you. This is a known area of success for you. Physically, you know what to do and you do it (You go to bed early). Mentally, you know what to do <u>and</u> you have an expectation of a positive outcome (I need to go to bed early because when I do, I usually wake up feeling better). Any words you might have about your cold are probably nonchalant which actually reinforces your actions, thoughts, feelings and expectations for a speedy recovery. You have experienced your recovery scenario a number of times and you probably have few, if any, opposing or negative thoughts about your quick recovery. Remember this ease and success and apply it to a different physical issue that you really want to improve. This helps you to manage your expectations and your outcomes. This adds clout to your prayers and affirmations.

Revamping your approach to life, i.e., laying the foundation for a new pathway of living, logically at first glance seems easy and it can be. Usually however, making way for new habits of living takes time and tons of practice, just as training for a new physical skill can also be a daunting process. In both mental and physical training, practiced repetition of any desired pattern and redirection of any routine at some point will transform into a seemingly auto-response. Everyone has their own personal tipping point. Typically, it takes effort and concrete reminders for any new skill to take hold, but this does not need to be the case. You can change things quickly depending upon the level to which you embrace your fundamental nature as a creator and by managing your expectations.

Younger generations may remember their essence more easily and develop these skills more rapidly and it is good to remember the generational assistance which paved the way for all of us. Regardless of age, dedicated practice and reminder mechanisms can support your preferred habits in the most direct manner. Post-it notes are still an all-time favorite reminder mechanism, as well as journal writing, intention setting, vision boards or safely lighting an intention candle as these methods engage your whole person. Today's technology provides great reminder tools such as affirmation apps, screen savers, phone timers, etc., with more tools being delivered to the marketplace regularly.

But whatever your preferred reminder method,
with dedicated practice there will be a moment when
your goal noticeably takes form and a choice point materializes within you.

At first you may simply observe an internal fork in the road offering a choice between your prior pattern and your desired pattern but carry on with your usual routine. Later you may have a stronger sense of a choice point for your preferred pattern and still choose to carry on with your old habit. Other times, you may actually take action in support of your new desired pattern. Then, there may be an occasional fluid choice response toward your new direction and then ever more frequently due to your efforts.

And one day, your preferred habit will seem to be on autopilot. You may experience a tangible lightness and ease with your prayer work that feels wonderfully delightful. But you need to keep working at it to avoid any erosion of your efforts.

Through your thoughtful choices and commitment, your preferred choice is now predominantly your auto-response and your old habit seems to be primarily replaced with your new habit. You may surprise yourself at first with an inner, "What was that?" or "Wow!" You may also find yourself thinking, "This is really easy!" followed by a "Why did I make it so hard?" or "Why did I make it take so long?"

There may also be occasions and even years when just for the heck of it, you choose to revert to your prior habits of living. **Conscious choice does require conscious focus.** It does get easier though as you develop your skills and expectations and the clarity of your prayers/affirmations will naturally evolve.

Changes

Once you make the decision to direct your path constructively and to reinforce your prayers by choosing mindful thoughts, words, feelings, actions and expectations, dramatic changes can be at your doorstep. Remarkably fast changes can be had when your actions, words, feelings, thoughts and expectations match your stated prayer/desire but you need to be willing to say "Yes" to the changes and be willing to make the internal move toward your new desired direction.

It is ever so easy to say "No" when new opportunities emerge. And you are only fooling yourself if you outwardly say "Yes" to the changes presenting themselves but don't internally support your desired changes with your thoughts, feelings and expectations. You may be receiving some sort of payoff if you use your words and actions to attest to the world that your efforts/prayers were a wasted endeavor when in actuality, you did not follow through internally with your thoughts, feelings and expectations. This last sentence is not to shame or blame but simply to give attention to possible current habits thwarting your way.

You need to trust when things do start to change so that you can move toward the direction that you desire. Find a way to make peace with any anxieties that emerge at this point or any point along your journey.

> **If you <u>fear</u> things will go backwards, they will.**
>
> **If you <u>look</u> for things to go backwards, they will.**

If your expectations are that of your prior pattern, you are directing things to return to what you did not want or to remain the same. No one else may sense this but you. This is where your internal honesty comes into play. If you can be frank about your true feelings and expectations, you have the opportunity to make and receive the changes you seek from your prayer work/affirmations. If you are ready to change out what is familiar to you but no longer serves you, you can make a new path and payoff for yourself. The opportunity is yours through your internal efforts.

Let's say you reversed a poor health pattern and are experiencing good health now. In reality, you may not actually be embracing your good health fully or even feel grateful for it. You may be filled with fear that you will not sustain your health. You may be scrutinizing every tiny or perceived negative change a hundred times a day and thus be looking for things to revert to the prior unwanted state. It is an understandable state to be in. It is a difficult place to be in and I encourage you to press on in the direction you desire.

Your prayers, i.e., your thoughts, words, actions, feelings and expectations…Your internal and external dialogues need to be aligned with your preferred outcome **at least the majority of the time.**

You really need to keep checking with yourself honestly, acknowledge what might be occurring internally that does not support your desire and redirect as needed. This is a long distance effort. This is your life journey. This is human development.

> Be honest with yourself.

Are you praying for one thing but expecting something else?

Or

Are there some things that are actually acceptable to you on some level and you are willing to live with as is?
Be honest about this too.
If so, make peace with where you are
and move on to something you <u>really</u> want to work on.

Life is a mystery and sometimes despite your best efforts, your goal is not received. This is where making a place within for peace and asking for guidance are just as important as your initial prayer. This is when letting go and releasing your prayer to God/Source for the best possible outcome is the next step to take.

Releasing to God is an active step not a passive one. Expressing your prayer is one step as a creator and opening your prayer to an outcome that you can't even imagine is another part of the equation. Managing your expectations is essential. Getting to a place where you know that no matter what, everything is okay now and will work out <u>is</u> mastery as a creator. Releasing your prayers/affirmations to God does not take you off the hook…you still need to actively direct your thoughts, words, feelings, actions and expectations constructively. It is a continual balancing act to say the least.

Being a Student

We are all students here. Be ever so kind and polite to yourself. Bring awareness to what is going on where you are at the moment, acknowledge it and switch out your expectations, thoughts, feelings, words and actions to match your prayer/desire as often as possible.

You are aiming to tip the scales of your patterning in favor of your constructive prayers.

Think in terms of baby steps, patience and commitment.

There is no room for blame, shame or guilt.

Dissolve all the "shoulds" away.

The analogy of peeling an onion is commonly used in the retraining process and with good reason. The word, frustration doesn't even begin to capture the feeling that may accompany your journey, but in my mind, ultimately worth every effort. I have so often kicked the onion analogy out of frustration when faced with yet another layer of personal challenges.

I hope you will stay the course,
even if you detour for years at a time.

Bring in love, acceptance, forgiveness and peace. Know that you matter. Ask for this. Expect this. Practice it. **And let it be.**

Change happens one choice at a time.

Partners in Action

We may ask angels, guides, Jesus, the Christ energy, God, Source, the Universe, the Life Force, the Creative Force, etc., for assistance when we pray for ourselves or others. And as we pray, we may also be prone to envision that there is some type of hierarchy in place…that angels, guides, Jesus, God, Source, etc., are higher on the food chain than we. We are not less than any of these life force expressions. We are made of the same stuff. So why not imagine we are equal partners before we pray?

Prayer is not meant to be a beseeching petition.
Prayer is meant to be a creative focus.

Take a deep breath and feel that difference.
As you imagine yourself to be an equal partner,
You become stronger in your confidence

GABRIELLE NUMAIR, MA

And your prayers develop in strength and clarity.

Be all that you really are.
Spread your wings and feel them.
Expand your awareness.
Be the fullness that is your birthright.
Let it in as much as you can in this moment.
Now, set your prayers forth.

With happiness and peace to you,
Gabrielle

TO SUPPORT WELL-BEING

MORNING INTENTION #1

Thank you for today.
Thank you for another chance to express myself as part of You, God/Source.
Thank you for the inspiration to direct my free will to create the happiest life ever.
Thank you for the guidance to know that what I think, feel, do, say and expect impacts me and the world.
Thank you for the awareness that the more I choose constructive thoughts, feelings, words, actions and expectations, the easier it becomes for me and everyone.

Change happens one choice at a time.
As I constructively feed our collective unconscious,
I impact what is possible for me and others.
Like a kaleidoscope, I change the sequencing of my life patterns through what I allow into my inner landscape.
My inner landscape feeds my outer landscape in every way and on all levels.

GABRIELLE NUMAIR, MA

Thank you for inspiring me in every moment to consciously train my mind to choose more uplifting thoughts, feelings, words, expectations and actions.
Thank you for supporting me to master this endeavor.

Amen/So Be It.

MORNING INTENTION #2

Thank you for today.
Thank you for the opportunity to see things differently.
Thank you for the opportunity to make way for things to be different.
Thank you for the opportunity to expect things to be different.
Thank you for the opportunity to do things differently.

For I hold the power in my hands to do so.

I desire to choose differently today.
I desire to make way for new and constructive habits
That will re-form my personal world and the entire world for the better.

Amen/So Be It
With thanks.

DAILY INTENTION FOR YOU

God surrounds me, my home and my car at all times
and in all ways.
Me, my home and my car are safe at all times and in all ways.
Through the grace and inspiration of God, I use my free will constructively to create the happiest life ever.

Amen.
Thank you.

DAILY INTENTION FOR ANOTHER

God surrounds ____, his/her home and car at all times and in all ways.
_____, his/her home and car are safe at all times
and in all ways.
Through the grace and inspiration of God, _____ uses his/her free will constructively to create the happiest life ever.

Amen.
Thank you.

BEDTIME INTENTION

Sleep well my body, host of my soul.
Thank you for framing my spirit so well.
Partners together, seeking our finest expression.
My desire is that we fully renew during this sleep.
Knowing we naturally link with Source for wholeness,
I support our alignment through my thoughts, words, feelings, deeds and expectations.
As I sing, you sing.
As I thrive, you thrive.
Thank you for knowing that my true desire is that you express vibrant health for me as you expand and develop in your expression as Source.
Thank you Body Electric Consciousness for knowing that you have an enduring right of way to express vibrant health for me, as you expand and develop in your expression of Source too.
I relax and rest knowing this is unfolding.
I relax and rest knowing this is unfolding.
I relax and rest knowing this is unfolding.

And so it is/Amen
With Thanks.

GUIDANCE FOR YOU

Angels be with me, may I feel your love.
Angels be with me, may I know my safety.
Angels be with me, may I understand your counsel.
Angels be with me, may I know my Source.
Angels be with me, may I embrace my true essence.
Angels be with me, may I realize my power.
Angels be with me, may I see what is possible.
Angels be with me, may I travel graceful paths.
Angels be with me, may I feel your love.
Angels be with me, may I know you are with me.
Amen. With thanks.

GUIDANCE FOR ANOTHER

Angels be with ____, may he/she feel your love.
Angels be with him, may he know his safety.
Angels be with him, may he understand your counsel.
Angels be with him, may he know his Source.
Angels be with him, may he embrace his essence
Angels be with him, may he realize his power.
Angels be with him, may he see what is possible.
Angels be with him, may he travel graceful paths.
Angels be with him, may he feel your love.
Angels be with him, may he know you are with him.
Amen. With thanks.

EXPANDING AWARENESS

God is ever loving, constant and unlimited.
I desire to expand my awareness of God's essence within me.
I now open to a broader and deeper understanding of God within me
in every area of my life.
I can rely on this because I desire this and by and large,
I grow in this expectation.
Amen. Thank You.

MAKING WAY FOR MY WELL-BEING

I relax into the well-being where my soul always resides.
I relax into the well-being where my body always resides.
I make way for my well-being through my thoughts, feelings, words, actions and expectations.
Amen/So Be It.
With thanks.

CONSCIOUS CREATOR #1

I Am My I AM presence here to explore and expand my expression of the Creative Force/God in me, as me and through me.

I desire the awareness of God/Source in me to grow every moment.

I walk in awareness as God intended.
I walk in conscious creation as God intended.
I walk in mastering constructive use of my free will as God intended.
I walk in love as God intended.
I walk in vibrant health as God intended.
I walk in abundance as God intended.
I walk in happiness as God intended.

For I Am My I AM presence and I consciously choose to focus in these directions.
And as I do so, I do it for others as well.

Amen/So Be It.
Thank you.

CONSTANCY OF SOURCE

I am the constant beauty of my soul.
I am the constant health of my soul.
I am the constant well-being of my soul.
I am the constant abundance of my soul.
I am the constant safety of my soul.
I am the constant unfolding of my soul.
I am the constant expanding of my awareness as God.

I, as Source, support me,
Knowing and acknowledging that I am Source Energy,
Complete and expanding.

Amen/And so it is.
With thanks.

DIRECTING MY EXPRESSION

I focus on my internal lane and stay in my inner lane because
That is my real and only job here…
To be the unique and creative expression of God/Source
In me, as me and through me.
Amen.

INTERNAL HEALTH

I focus on my internal health so that I may experience full and vibrant health in all my environments…physical, mental, spiritual and emotional.

Inspire me God to focus on my internal health so that I may experience full and vibrant health in the physical world and in all of my environments.

May thoughts and feelings of happiness, love, health, peace and abundance radiate through my mind.
May my predominant "go to" choices be those choices that nourish my well-being on all levels.

Thank you for my expanding mindfulness of what I am broadcasting to myself and to others.
Thank you for my ever increasing choice to steer my mind in more constructive directions.
Thank you for my growing awareness of what I am creating through my primary focus and for gently learning to focus on what I actually want to experience.
Amen/So Be It. Thank you.

TENDING MY GARDEN

I desire to find enjoyment in every day.
I desire to delight my heart every day.

And so,
I look at what makes me feel good every day.
I look at what makes my heart sing every day.

I count my blessings every day.
And I give thanks for it all.

With expectation for these habits to grow, thrive and continually evolve.
Making way for my happiness, well-being, vibrant health, love, abundance and creative expression to grow and expand every day.

Amen.
With thanks.

EXPECTING POSITIVE OUTCOMES

I desire to experience more positive outcomes in my daily life.
And so I make a habit to seek and to expect positive outcomes.

I cultivate this habit through my thoughts, words, feelings, actions and expectations.

I experience more positive outcomes because
I predominantly expect *positive outcomes.*

I now allow this habit to grow, thrive and continue.
With thanks, Amen.

CONSCIOUS CREATOR #2

I routinely define my desires as a conscious creator.
I then support my desires through my thoughts, words, feelings and actions.
Most importantly, I expect my desires to come into my experience.

I am just training my mind to focus in my desired directions.
Simple but rigorous.
As I do this for me,
I do this for others.
Amen.

MASTERING CONSTRUCTIVE USE OF MY FREE WILL

Happiness is mine as I make it so.
Forgiveness is mine as I make it so.
Health is mine as I make it so.
Prosperity is mine as I make it so.
Love is mine as I make it so.

I look at my expectations honestly.
I assess my expectations for personal meaning.
I release expectations that no longer have personal significance.
I establish expectations and outcomes that serve who I am now.
I establish expectations and outcomes that serve my current aspirations.

I look at my thoughts, words, feelings, actions and expectations for congruence with my desires.
I regularly adjust my thoughts, words, actions and expectations in the same way that a driver adjusts a steering wheel when driving…
Gently, regularly, consciously and eventually automatically,
I form constructive habits that go with the flow of life.
Always moving toward ease, empowerment, love, health, happiness and abundance.

GABRIELLE NUMAIR, MA

Just as it is intended.

Amen/So Be It.
With thanks.

LIFE'S GOODNESS

I desire to experience life's goodness.

I experience life's goodness in direct proportion

To my definition of life's goodness.

I experience life's goodness according to my belief and Expectation that life's goodness is possible for me.

Therefore, I clearly define what life's goodness means to me at this time.

I take the time to look at my beliefs and expectations of what is possible for me.

I expand my beliefs and expectations of what is possible for me,

For I desire to expect to experience life's goodness.

And so, I typically direct my thoughts, feelings, words, actions and expectations toward my picture of what life's goodness means to me.

And as I do this, I get on board with what God intended for us all.

I use my free will constructively.

Amen.

HAPPINESS

I desire to master creating and experiencing happiness.

I desire to expect to master creating and experiencing happiness.

I master creating and experiencing happiness in direct proportion to my steady expectation of feeling happy.

Therefore, I primarily direct my thoughts, words, actions, emotions and expectations toward my picture of happiness for me.

Amen.

TO SUPPORT EVERYDAY EVENTS

EMERGENCIES

Use- Whenever you hear a fire, medical or police siren; encounter a catastrophic situation, auto accident, tragic newsflash, personal emergency, etc.

This simple yet powerful constructive declaration assists any situation and covers most parties impacted. It aids in clearing up your personal energy field assisting you to move you from fear to calm and from vulnerability to peace. Such action on your part also:

- Helps everyone by not adding to the fear surrounding an emergency situation;
- Reinforces the pathway of well-being that others may feel and follow and
- Assists in expediting the restoration of balance.

This is an example of how you can influence daily life in a positive manner.

So instead of fermenting over the tragic car accident you just passed on the road, pray for those impacted, for those helping and for their loved ones:

GABRIELLE NUMAIR, MA

Bless those in need.

Bless the helpers.

Bless their loved ones.

May peace be restored.

Amen. With thanks.

TRANSFORMING A WORLD CRISIS

OR ANY PERSONAL CRISIS

Acknowledging that the more we fill our collective consciousness with constructive thoughts, the proportion of constructive thoughts surrounding us increases. Thus it becomes easier for all of us to discover and choose positive thoughts and actions. It becomes easier for us to receive and choose constructive thoughts and options for ourselves and our world:

May our hearts be calmed.
May our hearts be filled with peace.
May our hearts now open to love.

May we desire a benevolent solution to this situation.
May we seek a benevolent solution to this situation,
So that we may discover a benevolent solution to this situation.
Let us see our world gracefully on the other side of this situation.

And as we direct our thoughts toward a loving and peaceful future,
We ask for healing of this situation in and for ourselves;
We ask for healing of this situation in and for everyone,
Knowing all is possible as we open to graceful potentials.

GABRIELLE NUMAIR, MA

Hope is ours as we make it so.
Peace is ours as we make it so.
Love is ours as we make it so.

Amen/So be it.
With Thanks.

RELEASING HABITS OF FEAR AND ANXIETY

Dear Source,

I desire to feel peaceful and safe.
I desire to know that feeling peaceful and safe is possible.
I desire to know that feeling peaceful and safe is possible for me.

Assist me in releasing the habits of fear and anxiety
Pressing in on me.
I desire to see through these habits.
Guide me to feel and choose thoughts, feelings, words, actions and expectations which are in alignment with all that
You Are and I AM.
Strengthen my resolve.
Inspire me to create and choose constructive patterns of being more and more.

Stir me to feel deeper satisfaction in choosing beneficial paths.
Encourage me in building routines that help me thrive as I desire.
Diminish my cravings for that which no longer serves me.

GABRIELLE NUMAIR, MA

Help me to open the door to another way of being and living.
Aid me to see things differently,
For I desire to hear and follow your prompts to choose that which serves me happily.

I desire to feel peaceful and safe.

With appreciation for your constancy, Amen.

GROWING COOPERATIVE RELATIONSHIPS

There are times despite your most sincere efforts, the best path may be to bless a situation and move on. Obstructive or dishonest spouses/partners, family, friends, employers, etc., need not be tolerated. If you determine that it is time to let go of an unsupportive situation, make your finest effort to leave with all the love, forgiveness and self-forgiveness you can muster.

As you heal and develop, you may no longer need to continue certain relationships for you have learned whatever lesson was present there for you. If you do move on, be sure to positively define your next steps to fill the vacuum you just created in your life. You may know the saying, "As one door closes, another opens". A wise person first identifies the door she wishes to walk through; what is desired on the other side and then works to constructively maintain the new opportunity.

In abusive relationships, above all keep yourself and those in your care safe. Seek out and use available community resources to support your situation as needed.

I desire to experience cooperative relationships in all areas of my life.
Therefore, I become aware of my own unloving and unsupportive

thoughts, feelings, words, actions and expectations toward myself and therefore toward others.

I desire to release the need to experience unloving and unsupportive relationships.
Therefore, I identify the beliefs I hold of myself which are unloving and unsupportive.
And I make conscious efforts to release the beliefs which do not constructively serve me.

I desire to be treated with kindness and consideration.
Therefore, I treat myself internally and externally with kindness and consideration.

I desire to be respected and treated with respect.
Therefore, I respect myself and treat myself with respect.

I desire to collaborate with myself in creating cooperative relationships.
Therefore, I opt more and more to select constructive choices internally and externally.

As I embrace myself lovingly, others respond accordingly.

Cooperative and supportive relationships
Are mine in the external world,
As I make it so in my internal world.

With thanks, Amen.

ATTRACTING A WONDERFUL NEW HOME

In advance, define your wants and needs in a new home. Use positive descriptives vs. negative phrasing, e.g., we desire to live in a nurturing and safe neighborhood vs. we don't want to live in a neighborhood filled with neglect and crime.

Dear God,

You know my/our desire for a new home.
Match our needs with the perfect place.
Inspire us to recognize your promptings.
Bring a match into our awareness
That feels right for our next step.
Move us to take the steps to bring this into fruition.

With thanks, Amen and It is so.

SELLING A HOME/ATTRACTING AN IDEAL BUYER

Dear Home,

Thank you for all the comfort and shelter you provide me/us.
It seems right for us to move along to another abode.
We release our ties with you and open to the new opportunities that await us and you.
We open to the right and perfect buyer to come into our experience.
Knowing that the timing and other details will line up as we desire and allow,
Our inner alignment reflects in our outer world.

In gratitude, Amen.

HOUSE BLESSING

May this home be filled with love and health.
May this home be filled with happiness and prosperity.
May this home be a sanctuary and place of renewal.
May this home offer safekeeping and comfort.
May this home inspire awareness and understanding.

May the roof and walls be sturdy.
May the devices providing heat, water and daily ease be reliable.

May this home be a beacon of light and harmony.
May this home share encouragement and possibility.
May our neighbors feel welcomed by us and welcome us.

May this home be felt as the heart of life,
Extending itself with love to our neighborhood.

With thanks, Amen.

OPENING TO A NEW JOB

Dear God Source,

I desire a new job that fulfills and sustains me/us on all levels.
I desire to attract satisfying work that aids me in prospering internally and externally.

Match my desire with the ideal persons and situation.
Encourage my expectations toward greater possibilities.
Assist me in making my way easy.

Knowing this is done as I make it so.
With thanks, Amen.

OPENING TO A NEW CAREER

Dear God,

I desire to expand into a career that cultivates my natural gifts.
Assist me in identifying a path which feels welcoming to my being.
Guide me to hear your promptings in my soul.

Inspire me to take the internal and external steps
to develop and flourish.

My path is made clear, because I make it so.
With thanks, Amen.

LAUNCHING A SUCCESSFUL BUSINESS

Dear God-Source,

My heart prompts me/us to begin _____ business.
I desire this business to fulfill a need in our world
Which brings benefit to me and others.

Guide me in the design and establishment of this business.
I desire the path to be clear and flowing, abundant and natural.

With thanks, It Is So.

SUSTAINING A SUCCESSFUL BUSINESS

Recognize what benefits your business has provided/is providing to you and others. Then identify the path(s) you want your business to follow now. What do you want your business to accomplish now?

Dear Source,

Thank you for my/our _____ business.
Thank you for the benefits my business provides.
Thank you for the inspiration to develop the business further.

I desire my business to now achieve _____.
Inspire my inner and outer activities to fulfill my goals.
Assist me in managing my expectations toward attaining the outcomes I desire.

With thanks, Amen.

MINDFUL CONCEPTION

Dear God/Source,

I/we have the desire to exercise another aspect of the creative process.
We wish to extend our love to another in one of the deepest ways.
We wish to connect with, welcome, conceive and birth another aspect of You in this physical life.

Open the ways for us to achieve our desire.
Help us relax in the knowing that our desire is already accomplished.
Assist us in allowing for the process to unfold here and now.

We wish to be alert to our duty to assist the soul in our care
In realizing self-love and
In remembering his/her joyful reflection of and connection with the Source of All.
May we do so with patience and delight, through example and guidance.
As we do for ourselves, we do for another.

With thanks, Amen.

MINDFUL ADOPTION

Dear God Source,

I/we wish to adopt a child who is a wonderful match for us all.
As we call this match forth, we harmonize with this child's desire for love.
As we advance our desire deliberately.
Assist us all in allowing for this ideal match.
Help us in making the way clear and effortless.

We wish to be alert to our duty to assist the soul joining us
In realizing self-love and
In remembering her/his joyful reflection of and connection with the Source of All.
May we do so with patience and delight, through example and guidance.
As we do for ourselves, we do for another.

With thanks, Amen.

TO SUPPORT HEALTH

OVERALL HEALTHY PRACTICES

To best support your health and overall well-being, consider muting and turning your focus away from all media when commercials or advertisements for illness, medications, crisis and general vulnerability appear <u>or</u> change the station/channel completely. <u>Then</u> change your "internal station" to your picture of vibrant health for you.

Be very particular about what you let in out of self reverence and not out of fear. You are learning a new internal language of being and a new external way of being. Therefore, be as patient and persistent as you would when learning any new task.

WELCOMING VIBRANT HEALTH

I desire vibrant health.

I desire to know that vibrant health is possible.

I desire to know that vibrant health **is possible for me.**

I desire **to expect** vibrant health as my experience.

Knowing kindly and deeply that I receive vibrant health in direct proportion to my core belief of what is possible for me,

I extend a sincere welcome to vibrant health through my thoughts, words, actions, feelings and expectations.

Therefore I gently, systematically and primarily direct my thoughts, words, actions, emotions and expectations toward my picture of vibrant health for me.

With thanks,
Amen/It is so.

TRANSFORMING THE SITUATION

Okay body, let's transform this differently this time and go to a more comfortable level with this.
You know how this works, so work it.

Let's transform this to feeling good.
Let's transform this to wonderful health.

I desire to feel better.
I desire to feel good.
I desire to feel great.

I know that you are reaching out to the boundless flow of God's energy for balance.
I relax and rest knowing that this will unfold as I desire and
I make space for this realignment to occur.
I let it be, knowing that this is the most important action to take.
I relax and rest knowing it is done.
And I reap the rewards.

Thank you. Amen.

GRACIOUS THANKS

Thank you for my ever growing understanding of the inter-relationship between my body consciousness and my soul consciousness.

Thank you for my ever growing understanding of the inter-relationship between my emotions and my health.

Thank you for my ever-growing understanding of the inter-relationship between my thoughts, words, actions, feelings, expectations AND my experiences.

Thank you for my increasing action habit to steer things back toward my desired direction when I notice that I have gone off my desired course.

Thank you for it getting easier and easier to focus on what I want.

Thank you body for quickly turning toward health as my thoughts, words, actions, feelings and expectations turn toward health more and more.

Thank you Body Electric Consciousness for always knowing that you have a clear path from me to express vibrant health as you expand and develop in your expression of God.

Thank you mind for primarily choosing constructive thoughts.
Thank you mind for primarily using positive messaging.

Thank you body for only following directions for well-being.
Thank you body for only following directions for health.

Thank you for my increasing confidence that vibrant health is always possible for me.

Thank you for it getting easier and easier to imagine vibrant health as my confidence in the possibility of experiencing vibrant health grows daily.

Thank you for it getting easier to want, believe and expect vibrant health.

Thank you for it getting easier to want, believe, expect and experience _____ (Insert your own needs here, e.g., my cells redirect toward health; my cells restore to balance; lighter and shorter headaches, etc.)

And desiring and knowing that soon _____ (Insert your own needs here, e.g., disease, headaches, etc.) will disappear fully from my experience

And in its place,

Vibrant health is now made home in me
And is My Experience

For this is what I truly desire.
With thanks, Amen.

DEVELOPING HEALTHY EXPECTATIONS

Every day I desire my health to get better and better.
Therefore, I make a habit of expecting my health to improve every day.
My job is to have a picture of what I want my vibrant health to look like and feel like.
And so I create my picture of health now.
I keep my thoughts, feelings, words and expectations *primarily* aimed toward that picture of my vibrant health.

Every day I am more and more comfortable with being really healthy.
I can rely on vibrant health as I primarily keep my thoughts, words, feelings and expectations aimed toward vibrant health.
And so my duty is to keep my thoughts, words, feelings and expectations primarily aimed toward my picture of vibrant health for me.

Every day I am more and more comfortable with the freedom vibrant health affords me.
As my comfort grows, my expectations of health can grow.
And so my task is to build trust in the creative process by keeping my thoughts, words, feelings and expectations aimed *primarily* toward my picture of being wonderfully healthy.

I can rely on this because I desire it *and more often than not, I expect it to happen.*

Every day I am more and more comfortable with using my free will constructively.
I use my free will constructively because it is my preference to feel good.
I can rely on this because I desire it *and more often than not, I expect it.*

And so I develop the habit of using my free will constructively.
And I allow this habit to grow, thrive and continue.

With thanks, Amen/So Be It.

BLESSING OF MEDICINE, VITAMINS AND FOOD I

Dear Body,
Take what you need to thrive from this substance
And leave the rest.
Thank you.
Amen.

BLESSING OF MEDICINE, VITAMINS AND FOOD II

Dear Body,
Take what you need to thrive from this substance
And leave the rest to pass through me gently and easily.

Dear ____ (insert your specific medicine, vitamin or food),
Follow your intended purpose and assist my body in thriving.
With thanks. Amen.

BLESSING OF JUNK FOOD

Junk food has a negative connotation in many circles. We labeled it and we can un-label it, if we choose. We can benefit from un-labeling if our thoughts, feelings, words and expectations are in alignment with our image of health. Something to consider as we move in deeper understanding of our creative abilities:

Dear Body,
Let's unequivocally enjoy every morsel of this food.
Let's thrive from this food.
For in reality, whatever I think, feel, express and anticipate is what comes to pass.
Thrive from this substance
And leave the rest to pass through me gently and easily.

With thanks. Amen.

HEALING A MIGRAINE PATTERN*

*Or for any other unwanted health patterns you wish to transform by inserting your particular needs

I honor myself by focusing on what outcome I desire as a conscious creator.
I honor myself by allowing for healthy boundaries.
I honor myself by releasing guilt.
I honor myself by releasing any pressure or anger in a constructive way.
I honor myself by forgiving myself and others.
I honor myself by giving myself some slack.
I honor myself by loving and supporting myself.
I honor myself by imagining the freedom and comfort of vibrant health.
I honor myself by going with the flow of life within me.
I honor myself by opening to the expanding energy within me.

As a result,
It is getting easier and easier to focus on what I want.

It is getting easier and easier to desire migraines that are lighter and shorter in duration.
It is getting easier and easier to believe that migraines can be lighter and shorter in duration for me.
It is getting easier and easier to expect migraines that are lighter and shorter in duration for me.
It is also getting easier and easier to know that migraines can disappear from my experience because ultimately I desire it so and because I now make this possible for me.

It is just a retraining process that I am walking myself through on this particular subject.
Instead of calculating how long it's been since I've had a migraine and anticipating when the next migraine may appear,
I now express appreciation for my headache-free times and I express my desire for this healthy experience to continue.
I **seal** this desire by imagining my future as one that anticipates and experiences a great feeling body.

Vibrant health is mine for the asking as I keep making the mental fork in the road toward health and a migraine-free existence.
I am kind and gentle to myself during this process.

Anytime I notice my thoughts are veering off toward migraine expectations, I quickly and easily turn my thoughts toward expectations of health, ease and feeling good.
This action becomes as automatic for me as driving a car and noticing when I am veering off the road that will take me to my desired direction.

And if I do get a migraine, I am empowered to use whatever helpful aids and medications that support me back to feeling good.

I regularly remember to guide my mind toward
The life experience I desire.

This is the essence of the Life Handbook.
Simple, yet challenging. Possible and true.

I make my map and stick to it until
I am inspired to change my goal.
I refer to my map often to keep me on course.
I have confidence in my actions as a conscious creator.
I discern my empowerment as a beloved offspring of Source.
I honor my space moment to moment.

Thank you for it getting easier to want, believe, expect and experience lighter and shorter migraines.

Thank you for my healthy boundaries.
Thank you for letting go of guilt and anger.
Thank you for cutting myself some slack.
Thank you for releasing pressure and anger.
Thank you for forgiveness for myself and others.

Thank you for the confidence that soon migraines can disappear fully from my experience.

Thank you for the freedom of vibrant health.
Thank you for love and support.
Thank you for going with life's flow.
Thank you for opening to the expanding energy within me.
Thank you for my perfect feeling balance.

Amen.

CREATING AND EXPERIENCING VIBRANT HEALTH/MASTERING VIBRANT HEALTH

I desire to gain skill in creating and experiencing vibrant health.
I expect to gain skill in creating and experiencing vibrant health.
I master creating and experiencing vibrant health in direct proportion to my persistent anticipation of vibrant health.

Therefore, I release any and all expectations of ill health and/or fears of ill health.
And I gently direct my thoughts, words, feelings and expectations chiefly toward my picture of vibrant health for me.

Vibrant health is now made home in me.

I breathe deeply and allow calm and health to expand within me for this is my true desire.

With thanks, Amen/So Be It.

EASY ADD-IN HABITS

You can affirm the direction you wish your health and/or healing to continue by incorporating these few suggestions into your daily routine:

As you shower, give thanks for all of your body parts as you lather up. Here are some suggestions you can complete quickly during your bathing routine:
Thank you brain for being so sharp.
Thank you hair for growing so beautifully.
Thank you eyes for seeing so clearly.
Thank you nose and sinuses for breathing so easily.
Thank you teeth for chewing my food so well.
Thank you heart for beating so perfectly.
Thank you liver for detoxifying my body system.
Thank you kidneys for extracting wastes and balancing my bodily fluids.
Thank you lungs for my ease in breathing.
Thank you legs for being so sturdy and moving so gracefully.
Thank you hips for supporting my weight.
Thank you spine for enabling my movement.

Thank you hands, arms and shoulders for reaching, grasping, holding, pulling and other fun stuff.

Thank you feet for getting me where I want to go safely and with ease.

Thank you blood for carrying oxygen and nutrients throughout my system.

Thank you intestines for perfectly processing the food I take in.

Thank you _____ for _____.

When you climb or descend stairs:

Thank you legs and feet for keeping such perfect balance for me.

Thank you legs for your sturdiness and ease of movement.

Thank you feet for sensing any adjustments needed for balance.

Thank you knees for your flexibility and strength.

Thank you eyes for your keen depth perception.

Thank you _____ for _____.

NOTES ON EVOLVING EXPECTATIONS

You have to trust when things do start to change so that you can allow for and maintain your gains and move in the direction that you desire.

Don't look for things to go backward for if you do, you are directing things to return to what you did not want in the first place by your thoughts, words, actions, feelings and expectations (your internal and external dialogue).

<u>Keep checking your expectations and redirect them as needed.</u>

Be honest with yourself.

Are you asking for one thing but expecting something else?

Are you ready for these changes to take root?
How much are you willing to change?
What are you willing to change?
Are there things that you really don't mind enduring and so you really don't desire a change to take place?

Be ever so kind and polite to yourself.

Just acknowledge what is going on where you are at the moment and switch out your expectations to match your desire.

If there is something in your life that needs attention or is calling out for a change, address it.
All of the energy that you are using to avoid an issue or situation is diminishing you and your efforts.
There is no room for blame, guilt or shame.

Dissolve all the shoulds away.
Bring in love, acceptance, forgiveness and peace.
Know that you matter.
Ask for this.
Expect this.
Practice it.
Be thankful.
And let it be.

TO SUPPORT ABUNDANCE

WELCOMING FINANCIAL ABUNDANCE

I desire financial abundance.
I desire to know that financial abundance is possible.
I desire to know that financial abundance is possible for me.
I desire to know that financial abundance is right for me.
I desire to expect financial abundance as my experience.

Therefore, I discharge and release all thoughts, feelings, words, expectations and actions of personal lack or need for personal lack.
And in doing so, I make an opening for financial plenty in my life.
I now have an opportunity to believe financial abundance is possible for me.

In support of this opportunity, I regularly direct my thoughts, feelings, expectations, words and actions toward my picture of financial abundance for me.
I welcome financial abundance into my life.
I receive financial abundance in direct proportion to my belief and expectation of what is possible for me.
I receive financial abundance in direct proportion to my belief and expectation that abundance is proper for me.

GABRIELLE NUMAIR, MA

If I get off course and revert to past habits of lack or need for lack,
I easily get back on track by remembering my true desire for financial abundance.
I build habits that support my wealth every day

By looking at what is working well in my life,
By appreciating all that is currently in my life now,
By responsively caretaking all that I have,
By looking for more things to appreciate in the world,
By allowing for the mental and emotional space for more ease to enter my life and
By taking constructive action in the physical world to increase my wealth.

I ask my inner guidance to show me possibilities for easier pathways.
I hear and respond constructively to the guidance I receive.
These habits reinforce my desire and capacity for wealth in all areas of my life.

I desire and expect financial abundance to take root, grow and thrive in my life.
For I Am the Creative Force In Action as a Beloved Offspring of God-Source.
And I make room in my life for this growth to occur.

With thanks.
Amen and so it is.

MASTERING FINANCIAL EASE

I desire to master creating and experiencing financial ease.
I expect to master creating and experiencing financial ease.
I master creating and experiencing financial ease in
Direct Proportion to my Persistent Anticipation of Financial Ease.
Therefore, I direct my thoughts, feelings, words, actions and expectations **Primarily** toward my picture of financial ease.

Financial ease is mine to rely on more and more as
I Develop and Master these Habits of Living.

I am just re-training myself to think, feel, speak, act **and anticipate**
In the directions that I truly desire.
As I direct my free will toward my conscious desires more and more, I form new internal and external habits that support my goal of financial ease.

Thank you for my new habits that magnificently support my goal of financial ease.
Amen and so it is.

EXERCISING CONSCIOUS CREATION

Thank you finances for turning around quickly as my thoughts, feelings, words, actions and expectations turn toward abundance and well-being more and more.

It's just a natural progression toward more and more ease as I do my part by exercising my free will in positive directions.

I gain strength and confidence in my practice of conscious creation.

Thank you for it getting easier and easier to focus my energy in directions that feel good.
I am just retraining myself to go in directions that feel good to me.
I am creating new habits and in time these new habits will be my go-to routine.

I, as the off spring of God, make this so for,
I Am a Conscious Creator.

Amen and so it is.

TO SUPPORT A GRACIOUS TRANSITION

WHAT IS MEANT BY A GRACIOUS TRANSITION?

A gentle passing over; an easy letting go of our physical experience and opening more fully to our spiritual experience.

Why is this important to include?

It seems as if toward the end of our expected lifespan, many of us get caught up in the details of the physical world and don't seem to know how to let go, clinging to this world perhaps due to fear or lack of belief in the eternal nature of our souls. Others may try to remain out of a sense of duty. The reasons are as varied as we are.

Not everyone is like this. Some of us gracefully pass in our sleep or in another kindly manner. Some sense when their time is drawing near, embrace the coming transition and take action to clean up any loose ends including expressing their appreciation, making amends and sharing their hopes with those remaining.

Regardless, change isn't always easy. Birth and death are both sacred passages and life changes that deserve our respect. It puzzles me that as a society we offer considerable kind attention as we come into this life, especially in support of healthy childbearing and gentle childbirth but seem to withhold the same level of thoughtfulness as we prepare to exit this life.

When it comes to death, we tend to feel fear first. Fear for ourselves, fear for the dying and fear for life without our loved ones. We tend to be hopeful when a birth occurs. It seems naturally easier to embrace our entry passage with more mindfulness and respect. Perhaps our reactions to death are just learned behaviors. We have made some strides as a society in evolving our approach to death with the development of hospice care, books on death and dying, healthcare directives, grief counseling, etc. Beyond these advances, I suggest we provide more support to ourselves and loved ones as we prepare to exit physical life so that we might all experience greater inner peace and a more gracious transition.

Here is an example from my life to demonstrate my perspective:

My beloved grandmother was ill for about 7 years after a stroke. After hospitalization, she was cared for in her home primarily by my mom and her two sisters. Her doctor made regular home visits to see her, as did other medical personnel and church clergy. For the last months of her life, my grandmother was bedridden, mostly slept, remained curled up in a fetal position and began to develop gangrene on her feet. Her daughters took impeccable care of their mother round the clock…regularly juicing fruits and vegetables and placing an extra bed in her room so that someone was always with her at night. However, it was clear to me for a long time that my grandmother was lingering on for her family, and especially for my mom. One day at the end of a visit, I told my mom it seemed it was my grandmother's time to pass over but that she was hanging on, especially for her. I suggested to my mom that she tell my grandmother that she and the family would be okay and that it was alright to go. Later that day after I had returned to my home, my mom called me to tell me of my grandmother's passing. My mom said that as she rested on the other bed in my grandmother's room, she verbally spoke the words I had shared earlier with her to my grandmother. My mom told me that just after speaking the words I had shared, my grandmother opened her eyes, took a deep exhale and passed over. It was that modest of an exchange and clearly significant. I feel there was a healing for my mom and grandmother in that moment. Each one moving on with their paths in a respectful and gentle way.

Life is a mystery. It certainly can be scaring stepping over into what appears to be the unknown. Love and duty can also extend strong holds of attachment to physical life. I feel we have a sacred responsibility to extend peace and reassurance to others in their time of need, to offer thanks to our bodies and open to release to God's greater plan for us. These prayers are shared with this intention.

GETTING READY PART I

Dear God/Source,

I don't know what your time table is for me but I think I am getting to the end of this human life experience.

If so, I desire a gracious passing over and even better,
A conscious passing through.

I desire time to get things in order, to make amends, to express appreciation and to say goodbye.
I desire to feel your presence and your love.
I desire to feel your guidance.
I desire to hear your guidance.
I desire to feel ease.
I desire to feel joy.
I desire to feel safe, knowing that all is well.

Exhaling from my physical awareness and inhaling my eternal awareness is a transition that is meant to be
And meant to be graceful.

GABRIELLE NUMAIR, MA

Knowing that there is no delay between asking and receiving,
I open to your direction.

With thanks, Amen.

GETTING READY PART II

Dear Body,

I don't know what our time table is for sharing this human life experience but I think we are getting to the end of our journey.

Thank you for hosting my soul so well during this physical lifetime.
Thank you for showing up for me in all of the automatic ways that you do every day.
Thank you for all of the delights of human form.

It is with great sincerity that I state the following:

If it is our time to part ways, let us do so graciously and gently… peacefully and consciously.

If we are to journey longer together, let us also do so graciously and gently…peacefully and consciously.

If there is something that you need to thrive, let me know in one of the many ways communication is possible.

GABRIELLE NUMAIR, MA

If there is something that you need for release, let me know in one of the many ways communication is possible.

For we have been a team coming into and during this lifetime and I honor this relationship as I transition out of this physical experience.

May grace, peace, ease and comfort be ours.
With thanks. Amen.

FOR A LOVED ONE

Dear ___,

It seems like you are struggling so very hard to maintain your human experience.
It seems as if you are hanging on possibly because you are afraid to let go,
Or feel the need to stay to take care of ___ (me, others, etc.),
Or feel you have unfinished work to do,
Or even feel that this life you are now experiencing is all there is.

If it is your time to let go and return into the full awareness of Spirit/God,
There is really nothing to fear.
You are being cared for now and always.
It is okay to relax and let go.
It is okay to relax and step through with open eyes.
Spirit/God is holding you and will carry you as you let go of this physical world
And return your consciousness fully into spirit.
You will not go away. You will not cease.

GABRIELLE NUMAIR, MA

You will continue.

It can be as easy as a next breath.
It can be as easy as removing your hand from a glove.
It can be that easy.
It is that easy.

It is okay to let go.
I/we will be fine.
Everything will work out.
Thank you for everything you have done for me/us.
Thank you for _____.

Look closely and feel a gentleness surrounding you.
Look closely and feel familiar ones around you, guiding you, loving you.
Ask their assistance in letting go.
Feel their soothing embrace.
Give thanks for this human life.
Give thanks for your beautiful experiences.
Give thanks for your learning experiences.
Give thanks for your loved ones here in this physical life.
Give thanks for your next steps in this continuum of life that God created.

Your journey continues.
Allow yourself to let go.
Allow yourself to be with God consciously in all ways.

God blesses you always. Amen.

TO SUPPORT EVOLVING EXPECTATIONS

The following affirmation statements are shared with the goal of supporting the larger picture of your life…helping to keep your compass set toward your goals and to expand your capacity to receive that which you are.

QUICK SET-UP #1

Every day I am more and more comfortable with honoring my individuality.
Every day I am more and more comfortable with making constructive choices for myself.
Every day I am more and more comfortable with feeling safe and being safe.
Every day I am more and more comfortable with receiving encouraging support.
Every day I am more and more comfortable with feeling good.
Every day I am more and more comfortable with being healthy.
Every day I am more and more comfortable with having financial ease.
Every day I am more and more comfortable with having loving relationships.

Every day, more and more, I expect to honor my individuality.
Every day, more and more, I expect to make constructive choices for myself.
Every day, more and more, I expect to feel safe and be safe.
Every day, more and more, I expect to receive encouraging support.
Every day, more and more, I expect to feel good.

Every day, more and more, I expect to be healthier and healthier.
Every day, more and more, I expect to have financial ease.
Every day, more and more, I expect to have loving relationships.

Every day I honor my individuality.
Every day I make constructive choices for myself.
Every day I am safe.
Every day I receive encouraging support.
Every day I feel better.
Every day I am healthier and healthier.
Every day I experience greater financial ease.
Every day I experience loving relationships, giving and receiving love.

With thanks, Amen.

QUICK SET-UP #2

I desire to cultivate constructive use of my free will moment to moment.
And so, I build an awareness of my current patterns of thoughts, feelings, words, actions and expectations so that I can cultivate habits that are more beneficial to me.

I make a commitment to predominantly choose constructive thoughts, feelings, expectations, words and actions.
I make a commitment to predominantly exercise positive messaging, internally and externally.

Habits of constructive thinking, feeling, speaking, acting and expecting become second nature to me.

Beneficial patterns of thought, feeling, word, action and expectation become effortless to me.

I can rely on using my free will constructively because it is my preference.

And every day I am more and more comfortable with using my free will constructively.

I can rely on this because I desire it and more often than not, I expect it.

And so I develop a strong habit of using my free will constructively.

I allow this habit to grow, thrive and continue.

Amen. With thanks.

QUICK SET-UP #3

I honor the expression of God, the Creative Force through me, in me, as me.
I receive the fullness of what it means to be God's beloved offspring.
I feel the fullness of my soul now.

I am the grace and ease I desire to meet.
Be the grace that I am.

Amen/So Be It. With thanks.

QUICK SET-UP #4

Every day I am more and more comfortable connecting with my inner guidance.
I can communicate easily and clearly with my inner guidance
Because it is my innate rhythm to do so.

Therefore, I make a habit of quieting my mind and going within because it feels so good and provides so many benefits to me and by extension, the world.
I can rely on this because I desire it and more often than not, I expect it to happen.

I allow this habit to grow, thrive and continue.
With thanks. Amen.

YOUR INSPIRATIONS

ABOUT THE AUTHOR

Gabrielle Numair has been involved in spiritual pursuits since her teens. She shares prayers, affirmations and her perspectives in a straightforward and practical manner. Gabrielle encourages us to be empowered in our lives and to train ourselves to exercise our free will in a constructive manner.

Please visit www.totheheartofit.net for more information.

www.ingramcontent.com/pod-product-compliance
Lightning Source LLC
Chambersburg PA
CBHW030220100526
44584CB00014BA/1398